W9-BLC-816

On average, an

American mother

children

ime.

*A*s
anyone who has raised
children will attest,
motherhood is the
world's most intensive
course in Love.

—Katrina Kenison and
Kathleen Hirsch

M O M

*B*eing a
mother means learning
something new every
day, from healing cuts
with **kisses** to figuring
out how to wire money
across the country.

It was almost as though, in becoming a mother, I had joined an obscure religious sect, complete with rituals and rules and its own arcane vocabulary. Outsiders appeared suddenly peculiar, with their freedom, their laughter, their arms always unencumbered.

—Meg Wolitzer

MOM

Job description: Mother. Only patient, nurturing, protective women need apply. **Hours:** all. **Vacations:** none. **Benefits:** countless.

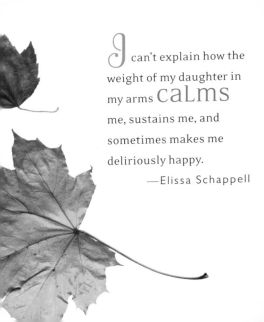

I can't explain how the weight of my daughter in my arms caLms me, sustains me, and sometimes makes me deliriously happy.

—Elissa Schappell

I, like most mothers, would KILL for my children. With a husband, it would depend on the mood I was in.

—Carly Simon

Nearly **three-quarters** of all the women living in America are mothers.

M O M

When you've got
kids to worry about,
a double bogey isn't the
end of the world.

—Myra Blackwelder

If we believe in ourselves the way our mothers do, we can do anything.

Nothing had prepared me for the tsunami of pure joy that hit me every time I rocked her to sleep, every time I held her in my arms.

—Susan Cheever

Being a Mother Means . . .

*L*earning the zen of

Letting go,

taking deep breaths, and

counting to ten . . . a lot.

—Sharon,

Washington, D.C.

Mothers are the

guardian angels

of humanity.

I would like my kids to know that they can do whatever they want and have a family and be an **accomplished** person in any walk of life.

—Juli Inkster

M O M

The **patience** of mothers is always being tested. First by temper tantrums, then by **driving lessons.**

$\mathcal{I}$ think one of the things my mom has worked at so hard and so successfully is being someone who really wants her daughter to do better than she did, to have more tools than she did, to have more opportunity, to understand boundaries better—all of that.

—Laura Dern

MOM

Mothers are the ultimate coaches. The better they prepare, equip, and train their teams the more likely their players will **succeed.**

29

$\mathcal{B}$abies need mothers. Sometimes lawyers, housewives, pilots, writers, and electricians also need mothers.

—Judith Viorst

M O M

We sat up and watched him breathe.

—Sharon Stone,
on her joy at having a new baby

Being a Mother Means . . .

You're constantly worried. You worry about everything from how warmly your children are dressed to what vegetables they're eating—even when they're all grown up and you don't want to concern them with your worries.

—Susanne, Sarasota, FL

3 3

The better a mother teaches her childre

e further they will Soar.

FOR THREE DAYS
EVERY MARCH THE
ANCIENT ROMANS

M O M

HELD A CELEBRATION
HONORING THEIR
MOTHERS.

37

Mother's Day was first celebrated in America on May 12, 1907. Seven years later President Woodrow Wilson declared it a national holiday.

When Mama talks, listen; it's the truth she's telling.

—Dorothy Allison

The doctors told
me I would never
walk, but my mother
told me I would—so I
beLieved
my mother.

—Wilma Rudolph

Some sort of silent trade takes place between mothers and children.

—Yuko Tsushima

Tears suddenly come to a mother's eyes when she watches her child be happy!

—Elizabeth Jolley

43

The best mothers

are those who *love* their children enough to let them fail now and then.

Being a Mother Means . . .

M O M

Getting as close to divine love
as is humanly possible.

—Cindy,
San Jose, CA

47

...the difference between being in Love with your baby and being in love with a man: When you're in love with a man, you don't pray for him not to call you.

—Alisa Kwitney

This tumult is life, and life
as a mother is one of its most
extreme forms.

—Constance Schraft

Motherhood is like Albania—you can't trust the descriptions in the books, you have to go there.

—Marni Jackson

MOM

$\mathcal{I}$f you can't remember
anything else at the store, **get**
Band-Aids.

Children see into the recesses of the soul. They are rarely fooled, seldom duped save at rummy and shell games. . . .

—Kaye Gibbons

My selfish reason for wanting to have kids is that—career or no career—I can't imagine anything lonelier than growing old and not having children to help make sense of my life.

—Kristin van Ogtrop

53

There is *no such thing*
as a

m t

MOM

ner

who doesn't work.

Flow simple a thing it

seems to me that to know

ourselves as

we are, we must know our

mothers' names.

—Alice Walker

M O M

My children are
my teachers.

—Jane Leavy

AMERICANS
SPEND OVER
$148 miLLion
ON **MOTHER'S
DAY CARDS**
EACH YEAR.

A mother's love is unconditional as well as eternal. It lives Long after her touch is gone.

59

It is a strange moment in our culture when we can speak of "deciding" to have a child, when truly we can no more "decide" to have a child than to decide to be born . . .

—Mona Simpson

M O M

How could I have spent so much time thinking about the birth process, and so little *envisioning* what might lie beyond it?

—Katrina Kenison

Mothering is a subtle art whose rhythm we collect and learn, as much from one another as by instinct.

—Louise Erdrich

It takes
strength,
compassion,
and wisdom
to be a mother
regardless of

whether you think
of yourself as

strong,

compassionate,

or wise.

In **2000,**
the average age of a
first-time
mother was
twenty-seven.

In 1980,

the average age was

twenty-four.

$\mathcal{I}$ couldn't leave my kids for a month. I know they'd probably be fine, but I don't want to miss anything.

—Susan Sarandon

What do you get on Mother's Day if you have kids? . . . A card with flowers that are made out of pink toilet paper—a lot of pink toilet paper. You get breakfast in bed. Then you get up and fix everybody else their breakfast. And then you go to the bathroom, and you are out of toilet paper.

—Liz Scott

Being a Mother Means . . .

*L*istening to a description of twenty-five different tricks on a skate-board and pretending you're really interested.

—Elaine, Ruxton, MD

71

ONCE A

m t

her,

ALWAYS IN LOVE.

Mothers have been **revered** since prehistoric times. The earliest sculptures in existence are those of Stone Age mothers-to-be.

M O M

The things that drive

a young mother to

exhaustion

are the very same

things that feed her

soul.

75

Did you ever meet a mother who's complained that her child phoned her too often? Me neither.

—Maureen Lipman

$\mathcal{B}$eing a **mother** meant put away your playthings and play house *for real.*

—Elissa Schappell

Good
mothers
ARE NEVER FREE.

There's a Love you can't experience until you have kids.

—Patricia Heaton

Set in Eidectic, Tarzana, Fling, and Gills Sans

Design and composition by
Diane Hobbing of
snapHaus Graphics

in Dumont, NJ